The Chocolate Marshmelephant Sundae

MIKE THALER

Scholastic Publications Ltd
in association with Pan Books

First published 1978 by Franklin Watts Ltd
This edition published 1980 by Pan Books Ltd,
Cavaye Place, London SW10 9PG
Scholastic Publications edition first published 1980
© Mike Thaler 1978
ISBN 0 330 26110 X
Reproduced, printed and bound in Great Britain by
Hazell Watson & Viney Ltd, Aylesbury, Bucks

TICKLETOON

WHAT DID THEY SAY?

Dr. Frankenstein

Julius Caesar

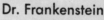

Christopher Columbus

animal instruments

A Violion

A Snake-saphone

A Pianoceros

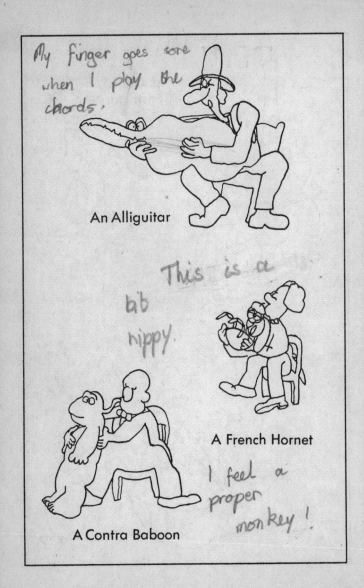

An Alliguitar

A French Hornet

A Contra Baboon

TICKLETOON

CRaZY CHaiRS

A Chair
Being Robbed

A Chair Doing
the Charleston

A Chair Thinking

A Chair Relaxing

A Chair
Praying

A Chair with
a Broken Arm

A Chair with
a Baby Chair

A Chair Imitating a Horse

funny food

A Hot Dog Bunny

A Chocolate
Marshmelephant
Sundae

A Gorilla
Cheese Sandwich

Can Riddles

1. What kind of can lives in Mexico?

2. What can was president
   of the United States?

3. What kind of can flies over
   the ocean and eats a lot of fish?

4. What do you call a happy can that
   lives in the United States?

5. What can is a monster?

6. What do you call a creature
   that eats cans?

7. What kind of can can you row in?

1. A Mexican

2. Lincan

3. A Pelican

4. A-merry-can

5. Frank-can-stein

6. A Cannibal

7. A Canoe

WHAT IS IT?

A chain smoker

A man driving
a nail

A Salt with a
deadly weapon

A bumper crop

A man having a light snack

The changing of the guard

THE THALER BOOK OF SILLY RECORDS

World's
best camouflaged
elephant

World's
flattest
mountain

World's
lowest bridge

WHAT DID THEY SAY?

Cinderella Bigfoot

or

IF THE SHOE FITS, WEAR IT.

Once upon a time
there was a girl
named Cinderella.

She lived
with her
stepsisters

and her
wicked
stepmother.

They were all very mean to Cinderella,

and she felt
very sad.

One day there arrived an invitation
to the prince's ball.

The wicked stepmother and the wicked
stepsisters spent weeks getting ready,

and on the night of the ball they left

So the fairy godmother
touched a silver teapot and a mouse
with her magic wand,

and he asked her to dance.

And they
danced

and they danced

and they danced.

Then the clock
struck twelve.

"I have to go,"
said Cinderella.

Cinderella got home just in time.

But the prince was determined to find her. So he tried the slipper on every maiden in the kingdom

with no luck

till he came to Cinderella's house.

Then he came to Cinderella

and the slipper fitted!

And they went away
and lived happily ever after.

the end

PICTURE POEMS

A snail playing
the tuba

A happy clam

A sad sky

A worm with
a question

The moon wearing sunglasses

A flower crying

A lightbulb with an idea

A cloud resting on top of a mountain

THE DAPPER CACTUS

TICKLETOON

WHAT IS IT?

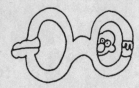

A man making
a spectacle
of himself

Attack at dawn

An old cow hand

A lady flying
off the handle

A man trying to
catch forty winks

A branch office

A man stamping
his feet

More Can Riddles

1. What kind of can can hop?

2. What kind of can makes
   the most noise?

3. What kind of can gives
   the most light?

4. What country has the
   most cans in it?

5. What kind of can rides
   a motorbike?

6. What do you call a prince
that's been changed into a can?

1. A cangaroo

2. A cannon

3. A candle

4. Canada

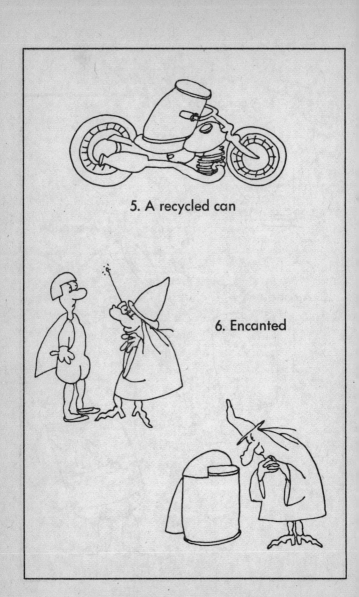

5. A recycled can

6. Encanted

alligator toothcare

two octopuses boxing

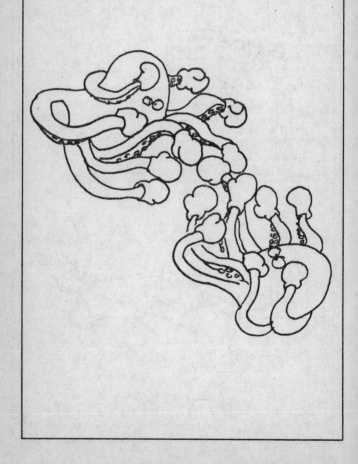

no bare feet

HOW DID THEY FEEL?

The man who fell in a  bottle?

The man who was run over by a steamroller?

FLATTERED

The girl who fell in a buzz saw?

BESIDE HERSELF

The girl who fell in the apple press?

BE CIDER SELF

YOU DON'T SAY

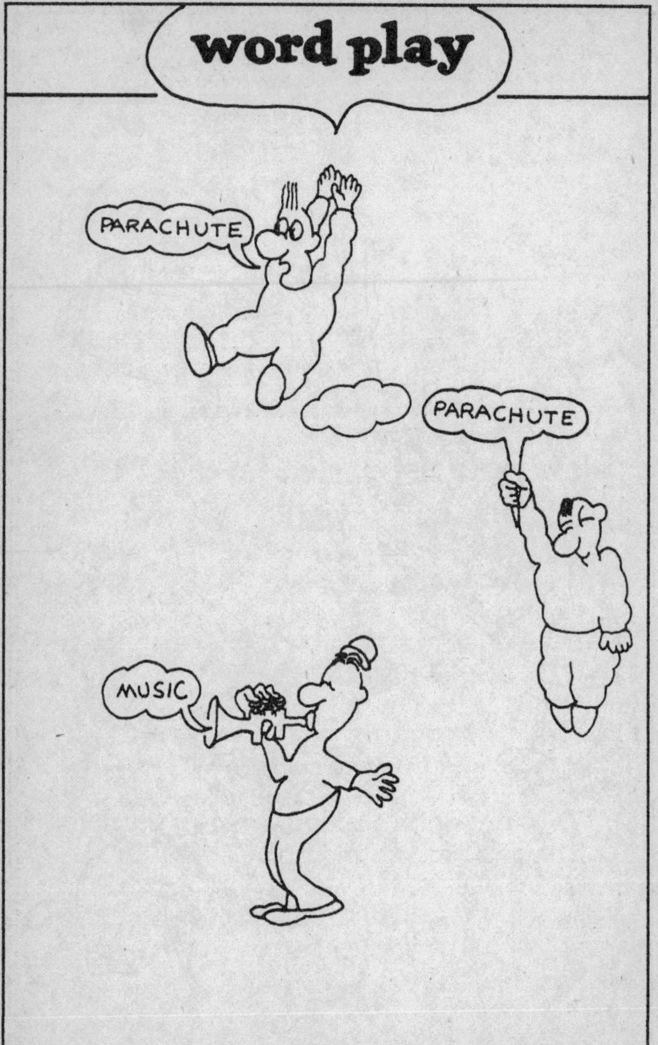
word play
PARACHUTE
PARACHUTE
MUSIC

Elephant Riddles

1. Who weighs 2000 lbs., ties his shirt in the middle, and sings "Day-O"?

2. What do you call an elephant that lives in Los Angeles?

3. How do elephants talk to each other?

4. What weighs 2000 lbs., comes in strawberry, raspberry, lemon and lime, and shakes?

5. What do you call a line of elephants that won't let you by?

6. What's green, has a long nose, and floats in a martini?

7. Who weighs 2000 lbs., wears a black leather jacket and says "AAAY"?

1. Harry Elephanty

2. An L.A. phant

3. On elephones

ELEPHONE BOOTH

4. Jellyphant

5. An elefence

6. An olivephant

7. The Elefonz

MEDICAL MISHAPS

SILLY SECTION

TICKLETOON

clouds

A cloud
resting

A cloud
eating a star

A cloud family

A cloud crowd

A shy cloud

are there?

Pencil-guins

Type-wrongers

Bottom hats

Unclelopes

Even More Can Riddles

1. What's the deepest can
   in the world?

2. What's the sweetest can
   in the world?

3. What can was a great conductor?

4. What do you call crazy cans?

5. What do you call a can that's been
   run over by a steamroller?

6. What can was a famous
   song-and-dance can?

7. What dance do French cans do?

1. The Grand Canyon

2. Candy

3. Toscanini

4. Repsychoed cans

5. Cancelled

6. Eddie Cantor

7. The cancan

THE WELL GROOMED CACTUS

ANOTHER SILLY SECTION

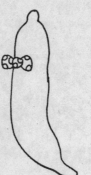

World's
best dressed
banana

THE EARLY WORM

Moral—The early worm gets the bird

more word play

MORE PICKLE RIDDLES

1. What pickle was a great composer?

2. What do you call it when
two pickles take a basket of food
into the country?

3. What is it called when
all the pickle athletes compete
against each other?

4. What do you call a pickle that
goes up and down on little wheels
at an amusement park?

5. What kind of pickle
knows how to swim?

6. What pickle pecks on wood
and is a famous cartoon hero?

1. Handill

2. A Picklenic

3. The Olympickles

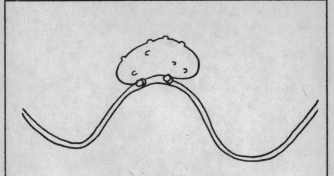

4. A roller Kosher

5. A dill pickerel

6. Woody Woodpickle